SCHOLASTIC

READ & RESPOND

Bringing the best books to life in the classroom

Activities based on Jasper's Beanstalk

By Nick Butterworth and Mick Inkpen

Terms and conditions

IMPORTANT – PERMITTED USE AND WARNINGS – READ CAREFULLY BEFORE USING

IF YOU ACCEPT THE ABOVE CONDITIONS YOU MAY PROCEED TO USE THE CD-ROM.

Recommended system requirements:
Windows: XP (Service Pack 3), Vista (Service Pack 2), Windows 7 or Windows 8 with 2.33GHz processor
Mac: OS 10.6 to 10.8 with Intel Core™ Duo processor
1GB RAM (recommended)
1024 x 768 Screen resolution
CD-ROM drive (24x speed recommended)
Adobe Reader (version 9 recommended for Mac users)
Broadband internet connections (for installation and updates)

For all technical support queries (including no CD drive), please phone Scholastic Customer Services on 0845 6039091.

C000228064

Designed using Adobe Indesign
Published by Scholastic Education, an imprint of Scholastic Ltd
Book End, Range Road, Witney, Oxfordshire, OX29 0YD
Registered office: Westfield Road, Southam, Warwickshire CV47 0RA

Printed and bound by Ashford Colour Press
© 2016 Scholastic Ltd
1 2 3 4 5 6 7 8 9 6 7 8 9 0 1 2 3 4 5

British Library Cataloguing-in-Publication Data
A catalogue record for this book is available from the British Library.
ISBN 978-1407-16058-0

Due to the nature of the web, we cannot guarantee the content or links of any site mentioned. We strongly recommend that teachers check websites before using them in the classroom.

Author Helen Lewis
Editorial team Rachel Morgan, Jenny Wilcox, Lucy Tritton, Rebecca Rothwell
Series designer Neil Salt
Designer Alice Duggan
Illustrator Cathy Hughes
Digital development Hannah Barnett, Phil Crothers and MWA Technologies Private Ltd

Acknowledgements
Every effort has been made to trace copyright holders for the works reproduced in this book, and the publishers apologise for any inadvertent omissions.

CONTENTS

INTRODUCTION

Read & Respond provides teaching ideas related to a specific children's book. The series focuses on best-loved books and brings you ways to use them to engage your class and enthuse them about reading.

The book is divided into different sections:

- **About the book and author:** gives you some background information about the book and the author.

- **Guided reading:** breaks the book down into sections and gives notes for using it with guided reading groups. A bookmark has been provided on page 10 containing comprehension questions. The children can be directed to refer to these as they read.

- **Shared reading:** provides extracts from the children's book with associated notes for focused work. There is also one non-fiction extract that relates to the children's book.

- **Phonics & spelling:** provides phonics and spelling work related to the children's book so you can teach these skills in context.

- **Plot, character & setting:** contains activity ideas focused on the plot, characters and the setting of the story.

- **Talk about it:** has speaking and listening activities related to the children's book. These activities may be based directly on the children's book or be broadly based on the themes and concepts of the story.

- **Get writing:** provides writing activities related to the children's book. These activities may be based directly on the children's book or be broadly based on the themes and concepts of the story.

- **Assessment:** contains short activities that will help you assess whether the children have understood concepts and curriculum objectives. They are designed to be informal activities to feed into your planning.

The activities follow the same format:

- **Objective:** the objective for the lesson. It will be based upon a curriculum objective, but will often be more specific to the focus being covered.

- **What you need:** a list of resources you need to teach the lesson, including digital resources (printable pages, interactive activities and media resources, see page 5).

- **What to do:** the activity notes.

- **Differentiation:** this is provided where specific and useful differentiation advice can be given to support and/or extend the learning in the activity. Differentiation by providing additional adult support has not been included as this will be at a teacher's discretion based upon specific children's needs and ability, as well as the availability of support.

The activities are numbered for reference within each section and should move through the text sequentially – so you can use the lesson while you are reading the book. Once you have read the book, most of the activities can be used in any order you wish.

Below are brief guidance notes for using the CD-ROM. For more detailed information, please click on the '?' button in the top right-hand corner of the screen.

The program contains the following:

- the extract pages from the book
- all of the photocopiable pages from the book
- additional printable pages
- interactive on-screen activities
- media resources.

Getting started

Put the CD-ROM into your CD-ROM drive. If you do not have a CD-ROM drive, phone Scholastic Customer Services on 0845 6039091.

- For Windows users, the install wizard should autorun, if it fails to do so then navigate to your CD-ROM drive. Then follow the installation process.
- For Mac users, copy the disk image file to your hard drive. After it has finished copying double click it to mount the disk image. Navigate to the mounted disk image and run the installer. After installation the disk image can be unmounted and the DMG can be deleted from the hard drive.
- To install on a network, see the ReadMe file located on the CD-ROM (navigate to your drive).

To complete the installation of the program you need to open the program and click 'Update' in the pop-up. Please note – this CD-ROM is web-enabled and the content will be downloaded from the internet to your hard drive to populate the CD-ROM with the relevant resources. This only needs to be done on first use after this you will be able to use the CD-ROM without an internet connection. If at any point any content is updated, you will receive another pop-up upon start-up when there is an internet connection.

Main menu

The main menu is the first screen that appears. Here you can access: terms and conditions, registration links, how to use the CD-ROM and credits. To access a specific book click on the relevant button (NB only titles installed will be available). You can filter by the

drop-down lists if you wish. You can search all resources by clicking 'Search' in the bottom left-hand corner. You can also log in and access favourites that you have bookmarked.

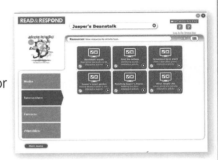

Resources

By clicking on a book on the Main menu, you are taken to the resources for that title. The resources are: Media, Interactives, Extracts and Printables. Select the category and then launch a resource by clicking the play button.

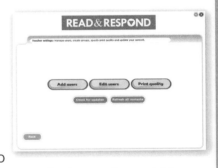

Teacher settings

In the top right-hand corner of the screen is a small 'T' icon. This is the teacher settings area. It is password protected, the password is: login. This area will allow you to choose the print quality settings for interactive activities ('Default' or 'Best') and also allow you to check for updates to the program or re-download all content to the disk via Refresh all content. You can also set up user logins so that you can save and access favourites. Once a user is set up, they can enter by clicking the login link underneath the 'T' and '?' buttons.

Search

You can access an all resources search by clicking the search button on the bottom left of the Main menu. You can search for activities by type (using the drop-down filter) or by keyword by typing into the box. You can then assign resources to your favourites area or launch them directly from the search area.

CURRICULUM LINKS

Section	Activity	Curriculum objectives
Guided reading		Comprehension: To develop pleasure in reading, be motivated to read, and develop vocabulary and understanding.
Shared reading	1	Comprehension: To make inferences on the basis of what is being said and done.
	2	Comprehension: To link what they read to their own experiences.
	3	Comprehension: To explain and discuss their understanding of what they have read.
Phonics & spelling	1	Word reading: To respond speedily with the correct sound to graphemes.
	2	Word reading: To read words with 'ed' endings.
	3	Word reading and Transcription: To segment spoken words into phonemes and represent these by graphemes.
	4	Word reading and Transcription: To read and spell words with the suffix 'ly'.
Plot, character & setting	1	Comprehension: To develop vocabulary.
	2	Comprehension: To make inferences.
	3	Comprehension: To discuss the sequence of events in books.
	4	Composition: To proofread writing to check for errors in spelling, grammar and punctuation.
	5	Spoken language: To participate actively in collaborative conversations.
	6	Comprehension: To retell a story.
Talk about it	1	Spoken language: To give well-structured narratives.
	2	Spoken language: To use spoken language to explore ideas.
	3	Spoken language: To participate in discussion.
	4	Spoken language: To ask relevant questions.
	5	Spoken language: To participate in a performance.
	6	Spoken language: To participate in role play and improvisation.
Get writing	1	Handwriting: To form lower-case letters of the correct size relative to one another.
	2	Composition: To write for different purposes.
	3	Spelling: To segment spoken words into phonemes and represent these by graphemes, spelling many correctly.
	4	Composition: To consider what they are going to write before beginning by writing down key words, including new vocabulary.
	5	Composition: To consider what they are going to write before beginning by writing down ideas, including new vocabulary.
	6	Composition: To write narratives.
Assessment	1	Comprehension: To answer and ask questions about the books they read.
	2	Comprehension: To explain and discuss their understanding of books.
	3	Comprehension: To retell a story.
	4	Comprehension: To participate in discussions about books.

About the book

When Jasper the cat finds a bean in the garden, he plants it, in the hope that it will grow into a beanstalk. Every day, Jasper tends to the bean enthusiastically. After a week, when the bean still shows no signs of growing, Jasper becomes disheartened. He digs up the bean and throws it away in disgust. Eventually, the bean grows into a beanstalk, and Jasper climbs up it to look for giants. *Jasper's Beanstalk* is a charming picture book that has won the hearts of several generations of parents and children since it was first published in the early 1990s. The story is very short (only 92 words) and the text is laid out sparingly, with just one sentence per double-page spread. The language is simple and follows predictable patterns, making it ideal for children just beginning to read independently. The story builds on children's familiarity with fairy tales (specifically 'Jack and the Beanstalk'). It also incorporates cross-curricular links. The narrative is structured around the days of the week, which links to attainment targets in the Year 1 programme of study in mathematics. The concept of growing plants from seeds and finding out what plants need in order to grow, links to attainment targets in the Year 2 programme of study in science.

About the author and illustrator

After leaving school, Nick Butterworth worked as a typographic designer and formed a partnership with Mick Inkpen. Nick is the author of many internationally acclaimed children's books including *Jingle Bells, QPootle5, Tiger* and *The Whisperer,* which won the Gold Award in the Nestlé Children's Book Prize in 2005. Nick's books have sold over 12 million copies around the world in more than 25 languages. Perhaps his best-known character, Percy the Park Keeper, first appeared in 1989 in *One Snowy Night* and has been the subject of a series of animated films for television. As well as writing and illustrating children's books, Nick has presented children's stories on television, created a cartoon strip for *The Sunday Express* magazine and worked for major graphic design consultancies.

Mick Inkpen is one of the top-selling picture book artists and writers in the world and is consistently in the top ten most borrowed authors in UK libraries. The *Kipper* and *Wibbly Pig* stories have millions of readers worldwide. He has won the British Book Award twice for *Lullabyhullaballoo* and *Penguin Small* and the Children's Book Award for *Threadbear.* He has also been shortlisted for the Kate Greenaway Medal and the Nestlé Smarties Book Prize three times, winning bronze for *Wibbly Pig's Silly Big Bear.* In addition to this, *Kipper* won a BAFTA for best animated children's film in 1998.

Key facts

Jasper's Beanstalk

Authors and illustrators: Nick Butterworth and Mick Inkpen

First published: 1992

Did you know? Nick and Mick grew up together in Romford and have been lifelong friends. Other titles they have collaborated on include *Just Like Jasper, The Nativity Play, The Sports Day, The School Trip* and *Wonderful Earth.*

▼ GUIDED READING

Cover story

Before you begin reading the story, look at the front cover of the book with the class. Ask: *What is the title of this book?* Together discuss question 1 on the Guided Reading bookmark (page 10): *Does the title of the book remind you of anything? If so, what?* Ask: *Who do you think the main character is?* (Jasper, who is a cat) *What can you tell about Jasper from the picture? What do you think the story might be about?*

Discuss the blue label on the front cover, which explains that the book is by the creators of *Percy The Park Keeper* and *Wibbly Pig*. Ask children whether they have read any books about Percy the Park Keeper or Wibbly Pig, and if so, what they thought of them. Ask: *Why do you think the publisher put this label on the front of the book?*

Draw children's attention to question 2 on the bookmark: *What do you think will happen in this story? Why?* Organise children into pairs to discuss this question, and then bring the class back together to share ideas.

Getting started

Open the book to the first page, with the text 'This book belongs to:...' Ask: *What is the dotted line for?* Draw children's attention to the picture on this page. Ask: *What book is Jasper reading? What happened in the story of 'Jack and the Beanstalk'?*

Turn over the page to reveal the first double-page spread. Together, read the text on the left-hand page, which lists more books by Nick Butterworth and Mick Inkpen. Ask: *Have you read any of these books?*

Turn over the page to show the second double-page spread that includes the title page. Read the title of the book together. Challenge children to sound out and read aloud the names of the authors.

Flip through the pages of the book that contain the story, discussing questions 5 and 6 on the bookmark: *The story uses large text. Can you suggest why? Look at how the text and pictures are arranged throughout the book. What patterns can you see?*

Waiting and waiting

Together, read the first three spreads of the story (from 'On Monday…' to 'On Wednesday…'). Ask: *Do you think Jasper is pleased to have found a bean? How do you know?* Together discuss Question 3 on the Guided Reading bookmark: *What do you think Jasper is hoping will happen when he plants the bean?* (The bean will grow into a beanstalk like the one in *Jack and the Beanstalk*.) Ask: *Why do you think Jasper put a stick in the place where he planted the bean?* (So that he would know where the bean is.) Ask: *Have you ever planted a bean? How did you look after it? Did it grow?*

Draw children's attention to question 8 on the bookmark: *How do the authors show the passing of time?* By using the days of the week ('On Monday…' and so on). Ask children to predict how the text on the next page will start ('On Thursday…').

Together, read the spread beginning 'On Thursday…' and discuss the meaning of any unfamiliar vocabulary, such as 'raked' and 'hoed'. Ask children to identify each object Jasper is carrying (a spade, a rake, a sprayer and a hoe) and match each object to the appropriate word in the text ('dug', 'raked', 'sprayed' and 'hoed'). Ask: *Why do you think Jasper did so many things to the bean on Thursday?* (He was starting to get impatient and he wanted to do everything he could to try to make the bean grow.)

Together, read the next three spreads beginning 'On Friday…' to 'On Sunday…' Ask: *Why do you* think Jasper picked up all the slugs and snails? (If his bean had started to grow, they would have eaten it.) *What happened when Jasper mowed the place where he'd planted the bean?* (The mower broke the stick Jasper was using to show where he had planted the bean.)

Together, discuss the following questions from the bookmark: question 11: *Why do you think the authors chose to make the main character a cat rather than a child?* Question 10: *Does Jasper make you laugh? What is funny about him?* and question 7: *Do you think the story would be as enjoyable without the pictures? Explain your answer.* Finally, ask children to predict what they think will happen next in the story.

....

A big surprise

Together, read the next two spreads beginning 'When Monday came around again…' and 'That bean…'. Discuss the use of speech marks to show the words Jasper said. Ask: *Do you think Jasper is right?*

Together, read the spread beginning 'But a long,…' Ask: *What happened to the bean after Jasper threw it away?* (The bean started growing.) *How long did it take the bean to grow?* (a very long time) *How do you know?* (The word 'long' is repeated.)

Together, read the spread beginning 'It did!' Ask: *What punctuation mark comes after the first two words on this page?* (an exclamation mark) *Why do you think the authors used an exclamation mark?* (to show that Jasper is delighted that the bean has grown into a beanstalk) Identify the pair of brackets on this page. Ask: *What do you notice about the words inside the brackets?* (They are smaller than the rest of the text.) *Why do you think this is?* (maybe to show that they are less important; maybe to emphasise the importance of the other two words on the page)

Together, read the spread beginning 'Now Jasper…' Ask: *Where do you think Jasper got the idea to look for giants?* (from the story 'Jack and the Beanstalk'.) *Why do you think there is an exclamation mark at the end of the sentence?* (because looking for giants is an exciting thing to do)

Together, discuss the following questions on the bookmark: question 4: *What do you think will happen after Jasper climbs the beanstalk?* and question 9: *Do you think the story has a moral (message)? If so, what do you think it is?*

Organise children into pairs or small groups to discuss question 12 on the bookmark: *Which is your favourite part of the story? Why?*

■SCHOLASTIC
READ&RESPOND
Bringing the best books to life in the classroom

Jasper's Beanstalk by Nick Butterworth & Mick Inkpen

Focus on... Meaning

1. Does the title of the book remind you of anything? If so, what?

2. What do you think will happen in this story? Why?

3. What do you think Jasper is hoping will happen when he plants the bean? Explain why you think this.

4. What do you think will happen after Jasper climbs the beanstalk?

Focus on... Organisation

5. The story uses large text. Can you suggest why?

6. Look at how the text and pictures are arranged throughout the book. What patterns can you see?

■SCHOLASTIC
READ&RESPOND
Bringing the best books to life in the classroom

Jasper's Beanstalk by Nick Butterworth & Mick Inkpen

Focus on... Language and features

7. Do you think the story would be as enjoyable without the pictures? Explain your answer.

8. How do the authors show the passing of time?

Focus on... Purpose, viewpoints and effects

9. Do you think the story has a moral (message)? If so, what do you think it is?

10. Does Jasper make you laugh? What is funny about him?

11. Why do you think the authors chose to make the main character a cat rather than a child?

12. Which is your favourite part of the story? Why?

Extract 1

- Display an enlarged copy of Extract 1 and read the first sentence together.
- Ask: *Why do you think the word 'waited' is repeated?* (To show that Jasper waited for what seemed like a very long time.)
- Ask: *How do you think Jasper felt?* (sad/disappointed/fed up/upset) *What makes you think Jasper felt like this?* (He was excited about growing a beanstalk/He had put a lot of time and trouble into trying to make the bean grow.)
- Read the second sentence together.
- Ask: *Why do you think Jasper dug up the bean? How do you think Jasper felt when he was digging up the bean?* (cross/angry/frustrated/impatient/intrigued) Ask the children to explain their thinking. They may reason they would feel that way if a similar thing happened to them.

Extract 2

- Display an enlarged copy of Extract 2 and read the first sentence together.
- Ask: *What did Jasper do with the bean?* (He threw it away.) *Why do you think Jasper did this?* (He thought it would never make a beanstalk.)
- Read the remaining text. Ask: *How do you think Jasper felt when he saw that the bean had grown into a beanstalk?* (surprised/delighted/excited/happy)
- Explain that Jasper thought that the thing he wanted to happen would never happen, but it did. Ask: *Can you remember a time when you thought something you wanted to happen would never happen, but in the end it did?* Encourage children to discuss this question with a talk partner.
- Ask selected children to share with the class what they have talked about with their talk partner.

Extract 3

- Display an enlarged copy of Extract 3.
- Read the title aloud together. Ask: *What type of text is this?* (non-fiction)
- Ask children to count how many times each of the following words appears in the text: 'bean', 'seed', 'plant' and 'soil'.
- Challenge individual children to come up and point to the following words in the text; as they do so, discuss the meaning of each word: 'swells', 'root', 'shoot' and 'pods'.
- Read through the text together once. On the second reading, give each sentence to a different child or group.
- Remove the copy of Extract 3 and display the interactive activity 'Growing a bean plant'.
- Ask children, working in pairs, to put the pictures from the media resource in the correct order and then to write a caption for each picture. You could give them copies of the printable page 'Growing a bean plant word mat' enlarged onto A3 paper.

Extract 1

On Sunday Jasper waited and
waited and waited...

When Monday came around
again he dug it up.

Extract 2

'That bean will never make a beanstalk,' said Jasper.

But a long, long, long time later...

It did!

(It was on a Thursday, I think.)

Extract 3

Growing a bean plant

1. A bean plant starts life as a bean seed.

2. A bean seed is planted in the soil.

3. Water from the soil soaks into the bean seed.

4. The bean seed swells and breaks open.

5. A root starts growing downwards.

6. A shoot starts growing upwards.

7. The shoot breaks through the soil. Two small leaves open out.

8. The bean plant grows taller. More leaves grow.

9. The bean plant grows flowers.

10. The bean plant grows seed pods. Inside the seed pods are the bean seeds.

PHONICS & SPELLING

1. Letters and sounds

Objective

To respond speedily with the correct sound to graphemes.

What you need

Printable page 'Speedy sounds cards', timers, interactive activity 'Find the letters', computers.

What to do

- Before the lesson, make a set of large cards from the printable page 'Speedy sounds cards'. Make enough sets of standard-sized cards to give one set for every three children.

- Tell children they are going to play some games using sounds from *Jasper's Beanstalk*, and the first game is called 'Speedy sounds'. Set a timer, and rapidly show the cards one at a time, challenging children to say the sound as quickly as they can. Stop the timer when children have correctly sounded out all the graphemes. Play another round of the game, challenging the class to beat their previous time.

- Organise children into groups of three, giving each group a set of cards and a timer. Ask children to play the 'Speedy sounds' game in their groups, with one child showing the cards, one child saying the sounds and one child keeping time. Swap roles.

- Tell children that in the next game they will be practising the same sounds as before, but that this game, 'Find the letters', is a bit harder. Display the interactive activity 'Find the letters', and demonstrate how to play.

- Give children an opportunity to play the game, either individually or in pairs.

Differentiation

Support: To give all children a chance to succeed, organise groups according to ability.
Extension: Ask children to devise their own game practising the same letter/sound combinations in the context of words.

2. What Jasper did

Objective

To read words with 'ed' endings.

What you need

Copy of *Jasper's Beanstalk*, interactive activity 'What Jasper did', blank cards.

What to do

- Ask: *What did Jasper do?* Challenge the children to identify the verbs (doing words) on the pages you are going to read.

- Together read the first seven spreads of the story, up to and including the spread that begins 'On Sunday…' After you have read each spread, ask children to identify the verbs. Compile a list of these: 'found', 'planted', 'watered', 'dug', 'raked', 'sprayed', 'hoed', 'picked' (up), 'mowed' and 'waited'.

- Ask: *What do you notice about how most of the verbs are written?* (most of them have the ending 'ed') Remind children that when you are talking about actions in the past, most verbs take the 'ed' ending.

- Show children the interactive activity 'What Jasper did'. Explain that the words and pictures show some more things that Jasper did. Challenge children to read the words and draw lines to match them to the pictures.

- Organise children into groups of four. Give each group a set of blank cards and a list of verbs in the past tense with 'ed' endings (such as, 'closed', 'shared', 'cleaned', 'followed', 'delivered', 'covered', 'helped', 'joined', 'picked', 'posted', 'pushed', 'signed', 'stopped', 'talked').

- Ask each child to choose, for example, three verbs. For each verb, ask them to make one word card and one picture card.

- Challenge groups to make up a game using the word cards and picture cards and then teach it to another group.

3. Jasper's word garden

Objective

To segment spoken words into phonemes and represent these by graphemes.

What you need

Interactive activity 'Jasper's word garden', computers, printable pages 'Word beginnings', 'Word middles' and 'Word endings', sticky tack, dictionaries.

What to do

- Before the lesson, make multiple sets of cards from the printable pages 'Word beginnings', 'Word middles' and 'Word endings' including one set of large cards. Colour the cards to distinguish between beginnings, middles and endings.

- Display the interactive activity 'Jasper's word garden'. Demonstrate how the game works, and build a few words together.

- Give children an opportunity to play the game, either individually or in pairs.

- Show children the set of large cards and explain your colour coding system. Display about half a dozen of each card colour on the board, with beginnings on the left, middles placed centrally and endings on the right.

- Ask a child to make a word by combining one beginning, one middle and one ending.

- Ask children to say the word aloud. Ask: *Is it a real word?* If it is, give the child one point. Ask: *Is it spelled correctly?* (Get children to check in a dictionary.) If it is they get a second point. Play a few rounds of this game, until children are familiar with it.

- Organise children into small groups to play the game, giving each group a set of cards and a dictionary.

4. How did Jasper do it?

Objective

To read and spell words with the suffix 'ly'.

What you need

Copies of *Jasper's Beanstalk*, sticky notes, dictionaries (optional).

What to do

- Ask a child to choose a page from *Jasper's Beanstalk* that shows Jasper doing something.

- Ask: *What did Jasper do on this page?* Using talk partners, ask children to suggest adverbs (words ending in 'ly') that might describe **how** Jasper did it.

- Come back together as a class and write the 'ly' words children suggest on the relevant page (for example, on sticky notes). Ask children for help with spelling each word.

- Organise the children into groups, giving each group a copy of *Jasper's Beanstalk* and some sticky notes. Ask each group to choose a different page of the book and repeat the activity. One or two children in the group could act as scribes, writing suggestions on sticky notes.

- Ask groups to swap books and sticky notes, and check each other's spellings. You might want to provide dictionaries.

- Help the children to create an illustrated display of their 'ly' words with the title *How did Jasper do it?*

Differentiation

Support: Group together children who struggle with spelling. Act as a scribe, but involve the children in writing as appropriate. For example, they could add the 'ly' ending to each word, or spell the whole word with support if the root word is short and phonically regular.
Extension: More able learners could act as scribes in the group activity.

PLOT, CHARACTER & SETTING

1. Words and pictures

Objective

To develop vocabulary.

What you need

Photocopiable page 20 'Picture cards', photocopiable page 21 'Word cards'.

What to do

- Before the lesson, make one set of large cards from photocopiable pages 20 and 21. Make one standard-sized set of cards for every four children.

- Show the large picture cards, one at a time, asking children to name each object. Establish the correct name for each object (as written on the word cards). Read the word cards one at a time.

- Use half the large cards to play a game of memory, arranging 12 picture cards face down in one grid and the matching word cards face down in another.

- Divide children into groups of four, giving each group a standard-sized set of cards. Ask children to play the memory game twice, once with each half of the deck.

- Ask each child to choose six words and learn to spell them using the look, say, cover, write, check method.

- Ask children to test each other on the spellings they have learned.

- Ask children to draw a picture of each word they have learned and then label it – without looking at the word card!

- Help children to create a display of their labelled pictures.

Differentiation

Support: Ask children to use fewer cards in the memory game (for example, eight per grid instead of 12). Ask them to learn to spell fewer words (for example, three instead of six).
Extension: Challenge children to learn to spell all 24 words on the cards.

2. Jasper's moods

Objective

To make inferences.

What you need

Large blank cards, copy of *Jasper's Beanstalk.*

Cross-curricular link

PSHE

What to do

- Before the lesson, create a set of large cards, each with a different mood written on it (for example, 'excited', 'worried', 'miserable', 'annoyed', 'surprised', 'delighted'). Avoid the words 'happy' and 'sad', as children tend to overuse these.

- Play a game of 'moody faces'. Show one of the mood cards and read the word together (for example, 'excited'). Say: *Show me an excited face!* Choose a child who has successfully made an excited face to come up to the front and show it. Repeat for the other mood cards.

- Display all the mood cards, re-reading them together.

- Read a page from *Jasper's Beanstalk* together. After you have read the page, point to a child and ask them to imagine they are Jasper. Ask: *How do you think Jasper is feeling?* Encourage the child to avoid using 'happy' or 'sad'. Challenge them to use a word from the mood cards or another appropriate word they know (for example, 'cross', 'upset'). Ask the same child: *What makes you think Jasper is feeling that way?*

- Repeat this activity for several pages from the book. Good pages for exploring contrasting moods are the pages starting 'On Monday…'; 'On Saturday…'; 'On Sunday…'; 'That bean…'; 'It did…'; and 'Now Jasper…'.

Differentiation

Extension: Ask pairs to choose a mood, and discuss these questions: What makes you feel that way? What does that mood feel like in your body? What do you usually do when you are in that mood?

3. Order it!

Objective

To discuss the sequence of events in books.

What you need

Copies of *Jasper's Beanstalk*, printable page 'Order it!', scissors, glue sticks, plain paper, one or two stories or rhymes based on days of the week (for example, traditional rhymes such as 'Monday's child', 'Solomon Grundy' and 'The Smoothing Iron' or picture books such as *The Very Hungry Caterpillar, Today is Monday* and *It's Monday, Mrs Jolly Bones!*).

What to do

- Organise children into pairs. Give each pair a copy of the printable page 'Order it!', a pair of scissors, a glue stick and a piece of plain paper. Challenge children to finish the sentences depending on what happened each day. Then ask them to cut out the sentences and put them in the right order, and then stick the ordered text onto the plain piece of paper.

- Bring the class back together and establish the correct order. Ask: *What clues did you use to help you work out the order?*

- Ask volunteers to read out their finished sentences.

- Read and discuss other stories or rhymes based on days of the week.

- Compare each rhyme or story to *Jasper's Beanstalk*, discussing similarities and differences.

Differentiation

Support: Give children copies of the printable page cut into eight sentences rather than 12, with the following sentences removed: 'That bean…', 'But a long…', 'It did…', 'Now Jasper…'.
Extension: Challenge children to write their own days of the week rhyme or story.

4. Fascinating facts

Objective

To proofread writing to check for errors in spelling, grammar and punctuation.

What you need

Copies of *Jasper's Beanstalk*, access to the internet.

Cross-curricular link

Science

What to do

- Give children a couple of minutes with partners to see if they can remember all the animals in the story.

- Ask children to check whether they have remembered all the animals by skimming through a copy of *Jasper's Beanstalk*.

- Make a list on the board of all the animals in the story: a cat, a robin, slugs, snails and earthworms.

- Invite children to ask questions about the animals. These could be generic questions that could be applied to any of the animals (for example, What does it eat?) or questions about specific animals (for example, Do robins build nests?). Write their questions on the board.

- Ask children to choose one of the animals and use their internet research skills to find out the answer to one of the questions. When they find out the answer they should make notes about it.

- Ask children to convert their notes into a 'fascinating fact' in the form of a sentence.

- Pair children to check each other's fascinating facts for errors in spelling, grammar and punctuation.

Differentiation

Support: Organise children into pairs for the research activity, with less confident learners paired with a more confident learner.
Extension: Challenge children to find out the answers to several questions and write several fascinating facts.

5. Build a beanstalk

Objective

To participate actively in collaborative conversations.

What you need

Copy of *Jasper's Beanstalk,* newspaper, sticky tape, scissors.

Cross-curricular link

Mathematics

What to do

- Display the page in *Jasper's Beanstalk* with Jasper looking at the beanstalk. Point out that the beanstalk is at least twice as tall as Jasper. Explain that a cat standing on its hind legs is about 60cm tall. Ask: *How high would a beanstalk be if it were twice as tall?* (120cm – about as tall as the children!)

- Challenge children to build a beanstalk that is at least as tall as they are.

- Show children the materials they will be using: newspaper, scissors and sticky tape. Explain any criteria you will be judging the beanstalks by in addition to height (for example, you might want them to be self-supporting).

- Organise children into groups. Explain that to work together well, they will need to talk to each other. Recap the rules for working in a group, for example, taking it in turns to talk; explaining what you think needs to be done and why; making joint decisions.

- As children are working, assess how well they are communicating. Encourage any children who are 'doing their own thing' to explain what they are doing and why to the rest of the group. Encourage any children who are struggling to ask a teammate for help. Help children to resolve any disagreements.

- Finish the session by judging the beanstalks. You could consider giving a prize to any group whose beanstalk meets your criteria.

6. Puppet performances

Objective

To retell a story.

What you need

Copies of *Jasper's Beanstalk,* interactive activity 'Retelling *Jasper's Beanstalk'*, thin card, colouring pencils, scissors, sticky tape, lolly sticks.

What to do

- Before the lesson, ask volunteers to draw the following: Jasper looking happy, Jasper looking sad, a robin, the bean, the beanstalk, a watering can, and a lawn mower. Cut out them out like puppets and tape a lolly stick onto the back of each puppet to act as a handle.

- Display interactive activity 'Retelling Jasper's Beanstalk' and challenge the children to retell the story while you fill in the boxes.

- Show children the puppets you have made and tell them they are going to make puppets like this to retell the story of *Jasper's Beanstalk.*

- Organise children into small groups. Give each group thin card, colouring pencils, scissors, sticky tape and lolly sticks. Give children time to draw, cut out and assemble the puppets.

- Give children time to rehearse their retelling of the story using the puppets.

- Pair groups up to watch each other's performances.

- Select one or two groups to give a performance to the whole class.

Differentiation

Support: Ask less confident learners to play the minor parts from the book.
Extension: Challenge children to elaborate on the story in their retelling, giving details that don't appear in the text.

Picture cards

● Cut out the cards.

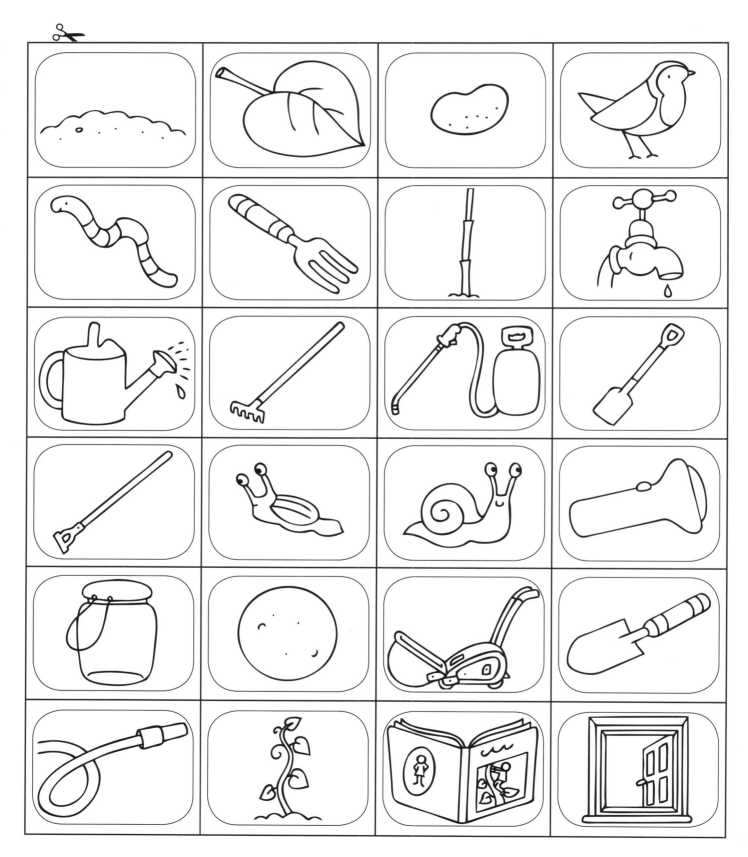

Word cards

- Cut out the cards.

bean	beanstalk	book	fork
hoe	hose	jar	leaf
Moon	mower	rake	robin
slug	snail	soil	spade
sprayer	stick	tap	torch
trowel	watering can	window	worm

▼ TALK ABOUT IT

1. Can't wait!

Objective

To give well-structured narratives.

What you need

Audio recording equipment (optional).

Cross-curricular link

PSHE

What to do

- Write the word 'impatient' on the board. Ask children what it means. (If you are feeling impatient it means you are finding it difficult to wait for something. You want things to happen faster.)

- Ask children if Jasper was impatient in the story. Establish that he was, because he found it difficult to wait. Ask: *What was Jasper waiting for? How did he show his impatience?*

- Ask: *What things do you sometimes have to wait for?* Get children to discuss this question with talk partners, and then share ideas with the rest of the class.

- Relate a story about a time in your own life when you had to wait for something and you found it really difficult.

- Ask children to think of a time in their lives when they had to wait for something and they found it really difficult, and to relate this story to their talk partner.

- Ask selected children to relate their stories to the whole class.

Differentiation

Extension: Challenge children to make audio recordings of each other's stories.

2. What would happen if…?

Objective

To use spoken language to explore ideas.

What you need

Photocopiable page 25 'What would happen if…? cards'.

Cross-curricular link

Philosophy

What to do

- Tell the children that they will be discussing some questions beginning 'What would happen if…?' Explain that the ideas for these questions came from the story *Jasper's Beanstalk*. Emphasise the fact that a 'right answer' isn't possible, and that you want children to use their imaginations.

- Organise the class into six groups, giving each group a different 'What would happen if…? card' from photocopiable page 25. Give children a set time (such as three minutes) to discuss the question on the card.

- When the time is up, ask each group to pass their card onto the next group. Give children the same length of time to discuss the new question they have received.

- Repeat this process until every group has discussed every question.

- Ask volunteers to share with the rest of the class some of the ideas they discussed in their group.

- Challenge children to devise their own questions beginning 'What would happen if…?' They don't necessarily need to be based on characters or events from *Jasper's Beanstalk*.

- Write the children's questions on the board.

- Organise children into pairs to choose and discuss one of the questions on the board.

- Ask children to draw a picture inspired by one of the questions they have discussed and to write a caption for it.

- Work with children to create a 'What would happen if…?' book containing captioned illustrations.

3. Taking care

Objective
To participate in discussion.

What you need
Copy of *Jasper's Beanstalk*, media resource 'Taking care'.

Cross-curricular link
PSHE, philosophy

What to do

- Together read the spreads in *Jasper's Beanstalk* from 'On Wednesday…' to 'On Saturday…' inclusive. Ask: *What did Jasper do to the bean? Why did he do all these things?* Establish that he was trying to take care of the bean. Ask: *What does it mean to take care of something?* Together agree on a definition of what taking care means, for example, giving something/someone what it/they need(s).

- One at a time, display the photographs from the media resource 'Taking care'. For each photograph, ask: *What might you do to take care of this?* Give children time to discuss this question with a partner before sharing their suggestions with the rest of the class. Establish that different things have different needs, so they need to be taken care of in different ways.

- Talk about a time when you had to take care of something, or something you currently take care of. Explain what you did/do to take care of it and how it made/makes you feel.

- Organise children into groups, asking them to tell each other about a personal experience of taking care of something and how it makes/made them feel.

- Invite a few volunteers to share their experiences with the class.

Differentiation
Extension: Ask children to discuss the following questions: Who takes care of you? In what ways do they take care of you? How does this make you feel?

4. Ask Jasper!

Objective
To ask relevant questions.

What you need
Cat toy or puppet (optional).

What to do

- Write a large question mark on the board. Ask: *What's this?* Tell children this is a clue to what they will be doing this lesson, and ask them to guess what it means.

- Reveal to children they are going to be asking questions in this lesson. Ask them to tell you as many question words as they can think of. Compile a list of question words on the board (for example, 'what', 'where', 'which', 'when', 'why', 'who', 'how').

- Tell children they are going to be meeting Jasper and asking him questions.

- Ask children to suggest a question they could ask Jasper. Write the question on the board, asking children for help with spelling and punctuation. Remind children that all questions end with a question mark.

- Organise children into pairs or small groups to prepare questions to ask Jasper.

- Conduct a question and answer hot-seat activity, with children asking Jasper their prepared questions. Jasper could be represented by a cat toy or puppet. The person controlling Jasper could be you, another adult, an older child who's familiar with the story, or even a child from the class.

Differentiation
Support: To enable less confident learners to participate more fully, put them in a pair rather than a group, and choose their partner carefully.
Extension: Challenge children to write seven questions to ask Jasper – each question beginning with a different question word.

TALK ABOUT IT

5. Singing Jasper

Objective

To participate in a performance.

What you need

Copies of *Jasper's Beanstalk,* percussion instruments (optional), film recording equipment (optional).

Cross-curricular link

Music

What to do

- Sing the story from the begining using a tune of your choice, asking children to listen and follow the text. You might want to use a pair of maracas to make it more lively.

- Sing the song all the way through a second time, encouraging the children to join in.

- Teach the children the song using by going through the book spread by spread. Ask the children to suggest actions to go with the words.

- Practise the song with the actions until children can sing it without your guidance or using the book.

- Ask children to add a musical accompaniment to the song using percussion instruments and/or body sounds such as clapping, stamping or finger clicking.

- If you have film recording equipment, you could record children singing and dancing and then play the recording back to help them evaluate their performance. Subsequent rehearsals can then address any issues the children identify.

- Put on a performance of the song for another class. You might like to make a film recording of the performance to share with a wider audience, for example, parents and grandparents.

6. Playing Jasper

Objective

To participate in role play and improvisation.

What you need

Copies of *Jasper's Beanstalk*.

What to do

- Display the picture of Jasper holding all of the garden equipment (spread 4). Ask: *What do you think the robin would say to Jasper if he could talk? What do you think Jasper would say in reply?*

- Display the picture on spread 6 where Jasper is mowing. Invite two children to have a conversation in role as Jasper and then Robin.

- Ask each child to draw Jasper's face on a piece of paper and a robin's face on the back of the page.

- Organise children into groups of four, giving each group a different spread from the book that features both Jasper and the robin.

- Ask the groups of four to organise themselves into two pairs. Partners decide who will play Jasper and who will play the robin. Pairs role-play a conversation between Jasper and the robin based on the picture they have chosen. They should hold their picture in front of their face. They then show their role play to the other pair in their group. Repeat the activity with pairs choosing a different picture and partners swapping roles.

- Ask selected pairs to show their role play to the rest of the class.

Differentiation

Extension: Challenge children to link role-play scenes together to form a fuller re-telling of the story.

What would happen if…? cards

● Cut out the cards.

What would happen if cats could read? 	What would happen if animals could talk? 
What would happen if plants grew much, much faster? 	What would happen if things did not fall to the ground when you dropped them? 
What would happen if all beans were magic?	What would happen if snails and slugs were the size of humans?  

GET WRITING

1. Jasper's bean

What to do

- Open *Jasper's Beanstalk* to the page beginning 'On Monday...' Say: *Jasper found the bean on the ground. How do you think it might have got there?* Give children a few minutes to discuss this question with a partner.

- Bring the class back together and invite children to share their ideas.

- Tell children you will be working together to write a poem about how Jasper's bean might have got there. On the board write the title 'Jasper's bean'. Start the first line of the poem with 'Maybe it…' Lead a shared writing session to write three or four lines of the poem, each starting with 'Maybe it…'.

- Organise children into groups to write further lines of the poem collaboratively.

- Bring the class back together, inviting each group to share one of the lines they have written. Add each of these lines to the poem on the board.

- Ask children to write out the poem for display, focusing on forming lower-case letters the correct size relative to one another.

- Help children to make a display of their poems.

2. How to plant beans

What to do

- Tell children they are going to plant beans to see if they will grow.

- Ask children to watch carefully as you demonstrate how to plant a bean:
  - Fill a plastic cup about half full with compost.
  - Dampen the compost.
  - Place three beans, evenly spaced, around the edge of the cup.
  - Cover the beans with about half a centimetre of potting compost.
  - Dampen the compost again.
  - Label the cup with your name and the date.

- Ask children to plant beans the way you showed them. When they have finished, ask them to wash their hands.

- Display the media resource 'How to plant beans'. Tell children they will be writing instructions to give to children in another class. Using the pictures in the media resource as a prompt, help children to verbally compose a set of instructions.

- Ask children, working in pairs, to write a full set of instructions for planting beans.

- Make copies of the instructions to give to children in other classes.

3. A letter to Jasper

Objective

To segment spoken words into phonemes and represent these by graphemes, spelling many correctly.

What you need

Copies of *Jasper's Beanstalk,* photocopiable page 29 'Jasper's letter', photocopiable page 30 'A letter to Jasper'.

What to do

- Open *Jasper's Beanstalk* to the page beginning 'On Sunday...' Explain that Jasper has tried everything he can think of to help the bean grow, but it's still not growing.

- Tell children Jasper has written a letter to the experts on a gardening programme asking them for help.

- Display an enlarged copy of photocopiable page 29 'Jasper's letter' and read it together. Ask: *What questions does Jasper ask?* Help children to find the questions and underline them.

- Ask children to imagine they are one of the gardening experts. Ask: *How would you answer Jasper's questions?* Ask children to discuss their ideas with a partner and then share them with the rest of the class.

- Together write the start of a letter in reply from the gardening experts to Jasper. Focus on spelling by segmenting spoken words into phonemes and representing these by graphemes.

- Ask children to copy the start of the letter onto photocopiable page 30 'A letter to Jasper', and then write the end of the letter themselves. Remind children to attempt to spell words by breaking spoken words up into separate sounds and writing a matching letter or group of letters for each sound.

Differentiation

Support: Ask children to write only one more sentence to finish the letter.

4. Beanstalk words

Objective

To consider what they are going to write before beginning by writing down key words, including new vocabulary.

What you need

An interesting object, interactive activity 'Beanstalk words'.

What to do

- Show children the interesting object you have brought in (for example, a patterned plate). Teach the game of 'Description ping-pong'. The game is played in pairs. One player says a sentence that describes a feature of the object (such as *It is round.*) The other player then has to describe something different about it (such as, *It has three cracks*). Players take it in turns to describe a different feature of the object. The aim of the game is to keep going as long as possible.

- Display the interactive activity 'Beanstalk words'. Pair up the children and ask them to play a game of 'Description ping-pong' about the beanstalk.

- Tell children you are going to work together to create a bank of words to describe the beanstalk. Demonstrate how to use the interactive activity, typing in a few words suggested by the children.

- Organise the children into groups, assigning each group a scribe. Ask children to jot down as many words as they can to describe the beanstalk. (The game of 'Description ping-pong' should have given them some ideas.)

- After the lesson, ask one or two volunteers from each group to add their group's words to the interactive activity. Correct any errors and save the screen for later use.

5. Plan a story

Objective

To consider what they are going to write before beginning by writing down key words, including new vocabulary.

What you need

Copy of *Jasper's Beanstalk*, printable page 'Plan a story'.

What to do

- Open *Jasper's Beanstalk* to the imprint page at the back of the book, which has an illustration of the beanstalk with Jasper's paw and tail disappearing up it.

- Ask: *What do you think might happen next?* Give children time to discuss ideas with a partner, and then ask selected pairs to share what they talked about.

- Discuss the meaning of the term 'sequel'. Tell children you are going to work together to plan a sequel to *Jasper's Beanstalk*.

- Display an enlarged copy of the printable page 'Plan a story'. Explain the concept of a working title, and ask children to help you give the sequel one. Tell them that when they plan their own story they can always change the title if they can think of a better one after they've finished the plan.

- Take children's suggestions for what could happen in the story then complete the first part of the story plan, drawing sketches to show characters and events, with arrows to show the flow of the story.

- Give out individual copies of the printable page for children to plan their own version of the story.

- Encourage children to review their working title in light of their completed plan and change the title if they want to, writing the new title on the line labelled 'Final title'.

6. Write a story

Objective

To write narratives.

What you need

An enlarged copy of the printable page 'Plan a story', a completed screen from the interactive activity 'Beanstalk words' from Lesson 4, children's completed story plans from Lesson 5.

What to do

- Before the lesson, complete your own story plan on an enlarged copy of the printable page 'Plan a story'. Display this together with the completed screen from the interactive activity 'Beanstalk words' (you will need to fill in the words suggested from Lesson 4).

- Tell children they will be using the words they collected and the plan they drew up to write a story that is a sequel to *Jasper's Beanstalk*.

- Talk through the whole of your story plan with the children. Model writing the first few sentences of the story, asking for children's help in choosing what to write. Demonstrate spelling words by first segmenting them into phonemes. Also explain punctuation choices, for example, *I need a capital letter here because it's the beginning of a sentence.*

- Give each child a copy of the completed word bank and ensure they all have their completed story plan.

- Give children the opportunity to rehearse what they are going to write by telling their story verbally to a partner.

- Finally, give children time to write their stories.

Differentiation

Support: You could ask children to tell their story verbally to an adult instead of a child, as an adult may be able to help them to draw out language and ideas.

Jasper's letter

● Read this letter written by Jasper.

The Garden

1 Spring Lane

Summerford

Monday 4 April

Dear Experts,

A week ago I found a bean in the garden, so I planted it.

I am looking after the bean very well, but it is not growing.

Please can you tell me why the bean is not growing? What should I do to make the bean grow?

Thank you for your help.

Yours faithfully,

Jasper T. Cat

A letter to Jasper

● Pretend you are a gardening expert and write a reply to Jasper's letter.

Radio House
TV Towers
London

Thursday 7 April

Dear Jasper,

_____

_____

_____

_____

_____

_____

_____

_____

Yours sincerely,

_____

(Chief Gardening Expert)

1. Questions, questions

Objective

To answer and ask questions about the books they read.

What you need

Copies of *Jasper's Beanstalk*.

What to do

- Before the lesson, write four questions about Jasper's Beanstalk on the board; for example: Which garden tools did Jasper use? When did Jasper find the bean? What was the first thing Jasper did to the bean after he planted it? Do you think Jasper had done much gardening before? Explain why you think this.

- Cover up all the questions.

- Reveal the first question and read it together.

- Ask children to discuss the question with a partner.

- Repeat for the other questions on the board, revealing and discussing one question at a time.

- Ask: *How many different ways can you think of to start a question?* Write children's ideas on the board.

- Ask children, working in pairs, to devise and write their own set of four questions about the story, using the question starters on the board as a jumping-off point. Provide copies of *Jasper's Beanstalk* for children to refer to.

- Group each pair with another pair to form a group of four, and ask each other the questions they have written.

- Bring the class back together, and ask a volunteer from each group of four to read out one of their group's questions. Write these questions on the board.

- Ask pairs to choose and discuss one of the questions on the board.

Differentiation

Support: Ask each pair to write two questions rather than four.

2. Interviews

Objective

To explain and discuss their understanding of books.

What you need

Audio recording equipment (optional), video recording equipment (optional).

What to do

- Tell children they will be interviewing each other to find out what their friends think of *Jasper's Beanstalk*. Establish that an interview involves asking and answering questions.

- Ask: *What do you need to write a question?* (A question word and a question mark.) Ask children to write these on the board.

- Work together to devise two interview questions. Model how to write each question, discussing spelling strategies and punctuation.

- Organise children into pairs to devise and write additional interview questions.

- Bring children back together to share the questions they have written. You might write any particularly interesting questions on the board.

- Model conducting an interview with a volunteer, each asking and answering one or two questions.

- Ask children to choose two or three interview questions, and pair up with a different partner to conduct an interview.

- If time, children could conduct a second interview, asking a different person the same questions.

Differentiation

Support: Once children have devised an interview question, they could make an audio recording of it instead of writing it down. They could then use the audio recording, paused after each question, to conduct the interview.
Extension: You could ask children to make video recordings of interviews and share them with another class to persuade them to read the book.

3. Retell the story

Objective

To retell a story.

What you need

Interactive activity 'Jasper's Beanstalk', computers.

Cross-curricular link

Computers

What to do

- Display the start screen of the interactive activity 'Jasper's Beanstalk'.

- Explain that you want them to tell the story but you do not expect them to use exactly the same words as the book; they should retell the story in their own words.

- Demonstrate clicking in the box and type in the text suggested by the children.

- Revise important keyboard skills, such as how to type a capital letter using the shift key, how to use the backspace key to undo what you have written, and how to type punctuation marks such as full stops, speech marks and exclamation marks.

- Demonstrate how to save the page when you are happy with it.

- Give children time, working individually or in pairs, to use the interactive activity to retell the story of *Jasper's Beanstalk*.

Differentiation

Support: Provide children with a copy of the book to help them to remember the original story.

4. Debate it!

Objective

To participate in discussions about books.

What you need

Copy of *Jasper's Beanstalk*.

Cross-curricular link

Philosophy

What to do

- Open a copy of *Jasper's Beanstalk* to the page beginning 'On Friday night…' Ask: *Why do you think Jasper picked up all the slugs and snails?* (To stop them eating the bean.)

- Ask: *Do you have any relatives who look after a garden? Have they ever talked about slugs and snails being a problem? What do they do to stop slugs and snails eating their plants?* Establish that there are many ways to get rid of slugs and snails and that most of these methods involve killing them.

- Ask: *Is it okay to kill slugs and snails and other animals that eat garden plants?* You might want to write this question on the board. Tell the children they will be debating this question.

- Ask children to form two groups: those who would answer 'yes' to the question, and those who would answer 'no'. Split each group into smaller discussion groups. Ask each discussion group to come up with three reasons why it is/isn't okay to kill slugs and snails.

- Hold an informal debate in which children from both sides present their arguments.

- At the end of the debate, ask children to reconsider their opinion. Ask: *Have you changed your answer to this question? If so, why?*

Differentiation

Extension: Ask children to come up with another question related to *Jasper's Beanstalk* and carry out an informal debate exploring it.